WINDSOR THEN

A PICTORIAL ESSAY OF
WINDSOR ONTARIO'S GLORIOUS PAST

FROM THE ARCHIVES OF
WALKERVILLE PUBLISHING INC.

WalkervillePublishing

Which dreams indeed are ambition,

for the very Substance of the ambitious

is merely the shadow of a dream.

William Shakespeare

Overleaf: More than 1,700 Ford Motor Company Workers gather for group photo during World War I.

Design and Photo Editing by Chris Edwards
Edited By Elaine Weeks

©2011 Walkerville Publishing Inc.

all rights reserved

To purchase reproductions of any these images, contact us at:

519-255-9898
chris@walkerville.com

At the dawn of the industrial era in the 19th century, the Border Cities running along the straits between Lakes Erie and St-Clair were little more than primitive outposts in what was then Upper Canada. Remarkably, this region would transform into a world-leader in manufacturing and engineering innovation, with a particular emphasis on automotive production.

Simultaneously, advances in photographic glass plate and printing technologies – particularly by Louis Daguerre and George Eastman – would afford future generations a means to go back in time to witness an incredibly accurate journey of days gone by, unprecedented in the annals of mankind.

One of the greatest photographers of his day, Henri Cartier-Bresson, noted:

> "Photographers deal in things which are continually vanishing and when they have vanished there is no contrivance on earth which can make them come back again."

This new catalogue of old images contain several photos taken by professional photographers who sold them for postcards (the most popular way to communicate before the telephone) or for special edition projects by the corporate giants of the day, particularly the Ford Motor Company and Hiram Walker & Sons, who seemed to have a sense of its place in history; others found their way into newspapers or commemorative books as "slices in time"; the remainder are a mishmash of studio portraits and personal snapshots from local family archives.

"Windsor Then" provides an important piece of the puzzle that connects to our past. You may recognize images from one of our previous works, including our highly popular but now defunct publications, "The Walkerville Times," and "The Times Magazine", as well as our best-selling books, "Best of the Times Magazine," (2004 and 2005 editions) and "Postcards from The Past: Windsor & The Border Cities."

A virtual treasure trove, these photos came into our possession from a variety of sources, including the Ford Motor Company Archives, Windsor's Community Museum, and Hiram Walker & Sons archives; but mostly they arrived via readers, including amateur historians Charlie Fox and Bernie Drouillard, who wished them placed into this "time capsule" for future generations to appreciate.

To that end, we hope you thoroughly enjoy your journey through our pictorial "wayback machine."

Visit us on the web to learn more about this region's colourful past:

windsorthenwindsornow.com

walkervilletimes.com

Windsor's Ferry Hill, foot of Ouellette and Sandwich (Riverside), 1910

Riverboat Captain and Crew, 1890s

Pleasure Steamer Tashmoo, Port of Detroit

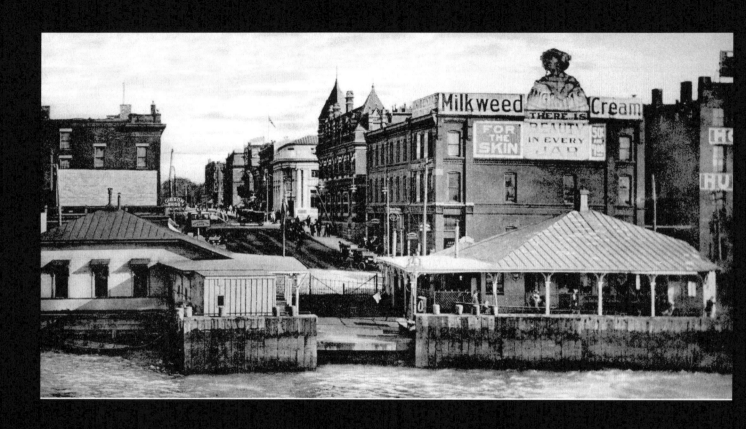

Windsor's Ferry Hill, 1910

Sinking Rail Tunnel Tubes, Detroit River, 1909

British American Hotel, Ferry Hill, Ouellette and Riverside, 1915

Parade Day, Windsor Armouries, 1906

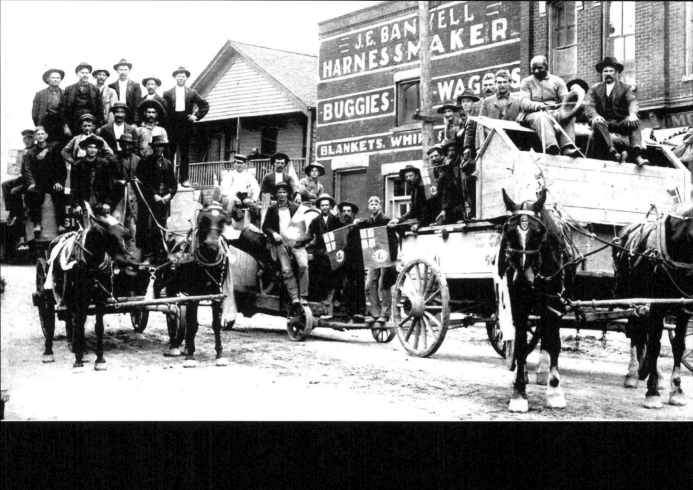

Moving Day, 1890s

Cooper, Hiram Walker & Sons

Car & Buggy, Hiram Walker & Sons

Canadian Club Bottling Line, 1899

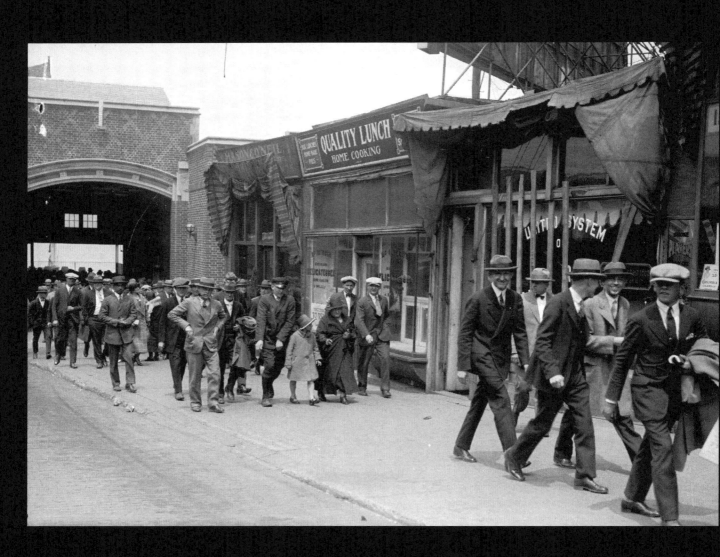

Crossing The Border to Ferry Hill, 1920s

Fill 'er Up Right on Pitt Street

Made in Walkerville
Seagraves Fire Truck

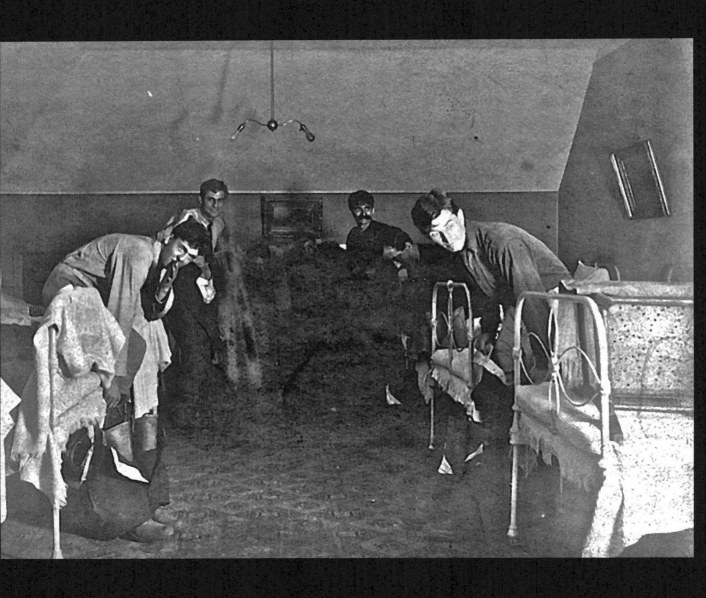

Up and At 'Em: Walkerville Fire Department, 1910

Off To World War I, Windsor Waterfront

Goodbye Kiss, WW I

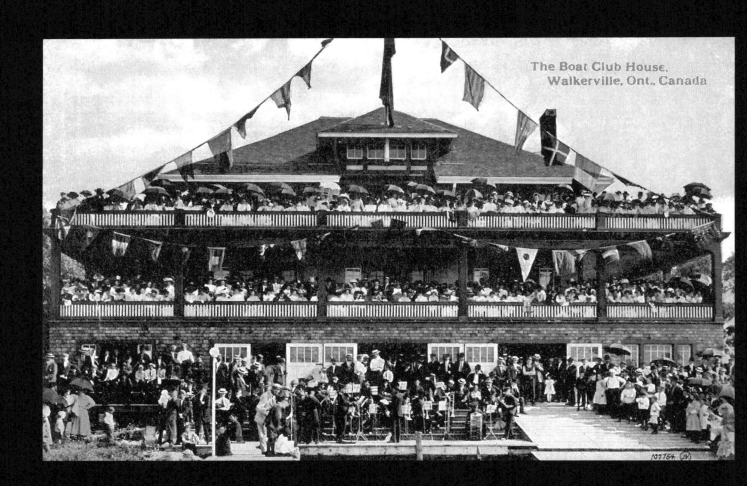

Team Ford

Ratchetheads, Ford Motor Company, 1910

Tow Job – The Sequel

Steve Paris, est. 1914, Pelissier Street

Last Ride

Ferry "Transfer II" Under Construction, Ecorse Michigan, 1904

Frank LaForet's Exchange Hotel - now The Victoria Tavern

Whisky Smuggling Man

Spoils of the Whisky Trade, Low-Martin House

Chasing Smugglers

THE BIG SCORE

The Force Be With You

END OF AN ERA

COOLING OFF IN THE DETROIT RIVER, 1930S

Dressed For The Occasion

A Tale of Two Cities, 1929

Campus Martius, Detroit, 1915

Raising Penobscot, Detroit

Retail Giants

Johnson Meat Market, Walkerville, 1920s

Canada Meat Packers Staff

Windsor Tool & Die, 1930s

Early Tool & Die Shop

Switchboard Operator

A Part of Factory District, Windsor, Canada.

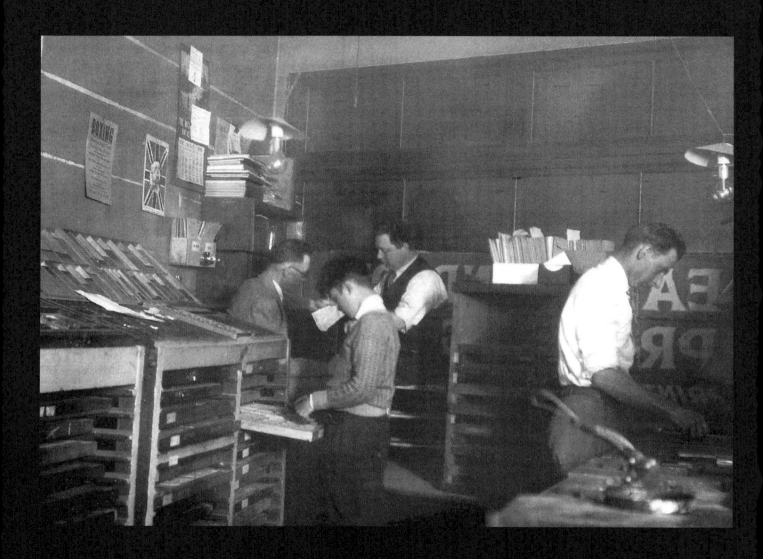

East Windsor Print Company

From Dirt To Concrete

Riveters, Ambassador Bridge, 1928

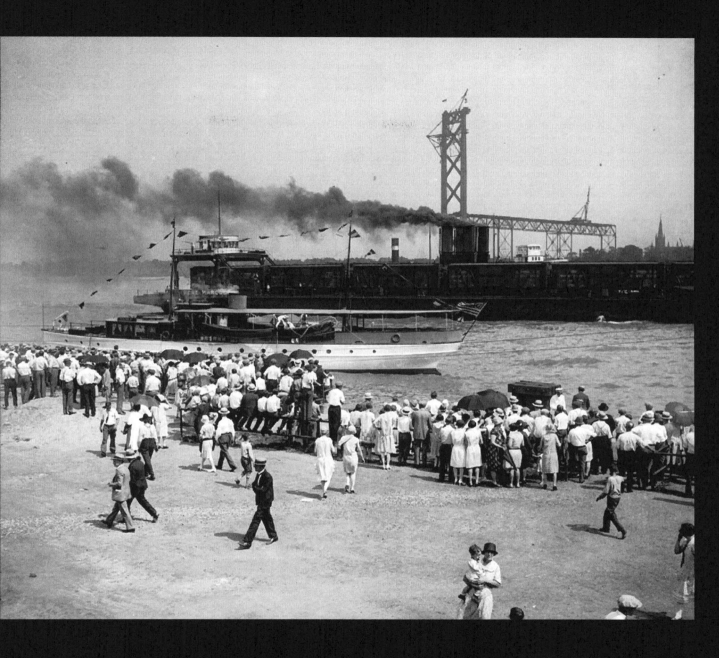

Ambassador Under Construction

Meet You in the Middle

Tightwire over Ferry Lansdowne

Flappers and Dancers, Boblo Island, 1920s

Detroit Docks, foot of Woodward, 1920s

Watermelon Boys

Mellowed in Wood

CLEAN TEAM

Walkerville Brewery Teamster at Memorial Park Gates, 1930s

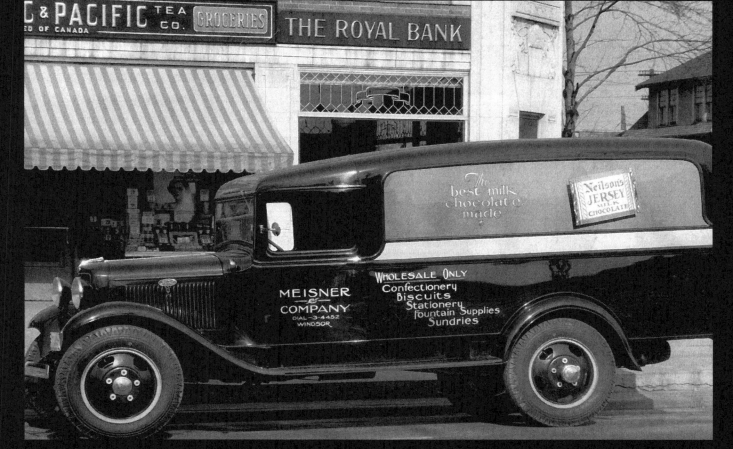

SW&A Terminal, University Avenue

Downtown Bus Depot, Chatham Street, 1940s

End of the Streetcar Era, 1940

Team CC

Made in Windsor Ford Jeeps Packed Off To War

The Peabody Building, Riverside at Chilver

Portrait of a Ford Worker

Ford Strike Along Riverside Drive at Drouillard Road

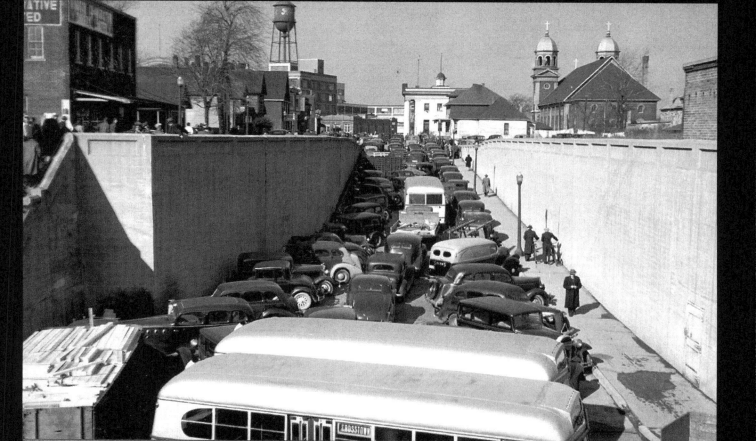

Buy Me a Mercury!

Tunnel Plaza, 1950s

Main Street, 1950s

End of An Era Along The Waterfront, 1950s

Queen Elizabeth Aboard The Britannia Tours Her Realm, 1950s

Walkerville, 1950

Made in the USA
San Bernardino, CA
28 October 2013